**P9-EEU-050**

## NEW from Kids for Saving Earth®

# AMAZING EARTH ADVENTURES

## A Kid's Guide to Preserving the Planet

By
The KSE Group
especially, Chapman Mott & Tessa Hill

KIDS FOR SAVING EARTH is an independent, nonprofit organization
dedicated to educating children about the environment.

SCHOLASTIC INC.
New York Toronto London Auckland Sydney

ISBN 0-590-45560-5

12 11 10 9 8 7 6 5 4 3                                    5 6 7/9

Printed in the U.S.A.                                    40

First Scholastic printing, March 1992

And this is the story of our
Amazing Earth Adventures...

How we found ways that
kids like us can help
protect the earth!

We hope you will enjoy our story
and get some good ideas for changing
things in your own neighborhood!

The earth needs your help,
too!

It all started one day at school. We were studying some of the problems on planet earth. We learned about air and water pollution, disappearing forests, endangered plants and animals like the whale and the panda. These are such big problems, even grown-ups have a hard time trying to solve them!

After class, Aly asked our teacher, "If adults can't solve these problems. . .

**WHAT CAN A COUPLE OF KIDS DO????"** And our teacher said, "Why don't you try to find out? You might be surprised!"

So Casey and I decided to team up and find out what we can do. And it turns out that a lot of the earth's problems are caused by people just like us! Instead of telling other people to clean up their act, we decided to fix our own problems first. We're just kids, but we found out that...

It took some time, and a lot of detective work, but we learned that we really can make a difference if we try. We can make the earth a better place!

At first, it was so confusing! We didn't know where to begin! Then my mom told us something that helped: Don't try to solve everything at once. Study one problem at a time and find a way to fix it. Then find another problem and solve it. Before you know it, you will be making a big difference!

So that's how we did it, one step at a time. It was a real adventure. And you know what? It was lots of fun, too! We hope you like our ideas, and we hope you come up with even better ones! The earth is the only planet we've got, and if we don't take care of it, who will?

# Earth Adventure #1:
# Trash or Treasure?

It was trash day in my neighborhood. Every house had several big bags full of trash out front. So we asked ourselves, "Where does all this stuff go?" The answer is, "To the landfill." Our teacher said that our city has nearly filled up three big landfills, and nobody wants the next one near their neighborhood. New land is expensive, and what about the animals that live there? Garbage also winds up in our parks, on our roadsides, and on our beaches. It costs money to clean it up, and injures fish and other water creatures who get tangled in it or mistake it for food.

There's only so much space on earth. So the answer to trash is not finding someplace else to put it. Instead of asking, "Where does it go?" we should be asking, "Where does it *come* from?" And the answer to that made us stop and think: a lot of garbage comes from kids, just like us!

# HOW MUCH TRASH CAN ONE KID MAKE?

## KIDS CAN HELP

To get an idea, we each kept a little notebook. We wrote down every single thing we threw in the trash during one week. (Try it, you'll be amazed!) Once we knew that we were part of the problem, it was easy to look for ways to be part of the solution, instead.

Here's Casey's trash list for one week:

6 aluminum drink cans
4 juice boxes
5 plastic cups
5 paper sacks
12 fast-food napkins
3 plastic forks
7 tin cans (cat food!)
2 old comic books
56 tissues (I had a cold)
4 dead batteries

and the list went on and on. . . .

Why don't you try making a trash list?

# THREE MAGIC WAYS TO MAKE LESS TRASH

So how can we make less trash? Three magic words gave us the clue: **PRECYCLE, REUSE, RECYCLE!** What do these magic words mean?

**"Precycle"** means buying things that have less packaging, last longer, or are reusable. It means *not* buying things that have too much packaging, or things that you use once and throw away, when something else would do the same job over and over again. Lots of places let you refill a glass or plastic cup with soft drinks. Every time you do that, it's one less disposable cup in the trash. Every time you use a metal fork or spoon, that's one less plastic one for the trash. Every real plate you use on a picnic is one less paper plate in the landfill.

## KIDS CAN HELP

"Hey, Aly, next time we go to the store, let's make a list of all the stuff with too much packaging. Then, let's talk to the store manager and show him the list. Maybe he'll start looking for products with less packaging."

"That's a great idea, Casey!"

cloth shopping bag

lunch box

refillable spray bottle

cloth napkin

ceramic mug

thermos bottle

sponge

rechargeable batteries

cloth hand towel

**"Reuse"** means finding ways to use stuff again and again, instead of just throwing it away. A paper bag can hold up for a week at least! A plastic lunch box can last for years! If you use a cloth shopping bag every time you shop, you cut down on the number of trees required to make paper bags, or the oil required to make the plastic ones! You save the energy and pollution making new bags will cause, and the landfill space to dispose of them. So reuse, whenever you can!

# KIDS CAN HELP

"Hey, Aly, let's make a display for school. Let's show all the kids some stuff that's reusable. Here, I made a list. . . ."

- Refillable spray dispensers, instead of disposable aerosol sprays.
- Sponges to clean up messes, instead of paper towels.
- Using both sides of every sheet of paper, then recycle it!
- Reusing envelopes, cardboard boxes, and wrapping paper.
- Using rechargeable batteries instead of throwaways. Batteries have lots of chemicals in them. Rechargeables can save money, and it's less to throw away.
- Using a reusable lunch sack or box.

**"Recycle"** means taking stuff that would otherwise be garbage, and using it to make new stuff instead. It saves money by cutting down on the garbage we have to move and bury. It costs less to make things from recycled stuff. And it cuts down on pollution! The biggest part of trash is paper, and recycling paper is easy. Plastic is harder to recycle, but that's catching on, too. Glass and aluminum are the easiest to recycle, because recycling companies can make money from them. In our town, recyclers will take glass or aluminum, but not plastic bottles, so we started buying all our drinks in glass bottles or aluminum cans instead. Your town may be different. You're a good detective, find out for yourself!

# KIDS CAN HELP

Try calling your City Hall and ask if they have recycling. If they don't, write letters to your city leaders to encourage them to start a recycling program.

## Be Creative About Recycling.

"Say, Casey, wouldn't it be wonderful if all the friends on our block would recycle. Let's talk with them about it and if they agree, let's make a Defender of the Planet Certificate for them. Let's draw it on the back of a used piece of paper."

## A WORD ABOUT WORDS!

When you're "talking trash," it's important to use the right words! Companies want their products to look "earth-friendly," because they know kids like us really care. But sometimes the words they use can be confusing.

Take these three words: **Recycle, Recycled, Recyclable.** They look a lot alike, but they mean three different things!

**Recycle** means making new things out of trash instead of throwing it in the landfill.

**Recycled** means a product made from stuff someone has already used, things that would have wound up in the landfill. This is a slippery word, sometimes. A lot of paper things that say "recycled," are really made from leftover scraps from the paper mill itself. So be sure to ask how much *post-consumer* waste is in the recycled products you buy. "Post-consumer" means someone else has used it at least once. The more "post-consumer" the better.

**Recyclable** just means the product *can be* recycled, *if* there is a place to recycle it. And if nobody recycles it, it doesn't make the earth a better place. It does not mean that it's made from recycled material.

# ONE KID'S TRASH IS ANOTHER KID'S TREASURE!

A good detective learns from others. "You know what, Casey? A cousin of mine from the country saw my dad stacking bags of old leaves and grass clippings on the sidewalk. She said, 'Wow, we could use all that stuff!' I asked her, 'What on earth for?' She said, 'Composting, of course!' " So Casey and I had another mystery to explore: How to recycle leaves and grass.

## Composting Solves Two Problems at Once.

Composting cuts down on the amount of trash in the landfill. And it cuts down on the chemical fertilizers we use on our lawns and our gardens. Composting is just nature's way of making dirt. And if you like to play with dirt, it's lots of fun!

# KIDS CAN HELP

## Here's the Basic Recipe for "Composting."

Put grass clippings and leaves and weeds in a big box (not cardboard), with spaces in the sides so air can get in, or if you don't have a big box, even a pile will do. Build stuff up in layers and wet it all down. Almost any kind of kitchen food scraps will mix right in. Even eggshells and coffee grounds are fine. But no paper, glass, or metal, of course. And it's better *not* to use meat, bones, or milk products (like cheese) since they tend to attract bugs. Mix some garden dirt in with the other stuff, and always put a layer of dirt on top, to help keep animals away. Keep adding to the compost heap, stirring it up and wetting it down. It may take several months, but nature will turn this trash into a great natural fertilizer. You can use it to mulch around plants in winter, or mix it with the soil in your garden.

YOU'LL BE SAVING MONEY, KEEPING CHEMICALS OUT OF THE SOIL, AND SAVING SPACE AT THE LANDFILL ALL AT ONCE!

# Earth Adventure #2: Energy Bandits!

The next problem we tackled was energy. Energy is a little tougher to understand than trash. You can see trash, but energy is invisible. You can only see what it does, like light your room or move your family car. The problem with energy is that every time we use it, we put pollution in the air, and that's a big problem for the planet!

## Where Energy Comes From:

Almost all the energy we use comes from plants. It's true! Plants take sunlight, food from the soil and water, and a chemical called "carbon dioxide" from the air, and turn them into leaves and stems. Even oil and gas and coal started out as tiny plants that lived thousands and thousands of years ago. That's why we call them "fossil fuels." We burn these fossil fuels to make electricity, to heat our homes, to run our cars and factories. The trouble is, every time we burn fuel we put carbon dioxide back into the air. And we're doing it a lot faster than the plants on earth can turn it back into leaves and stems! The extra carbon dioxide in the air is like the windows in your car: It lets sunlight in but traps the heat. And this is beginning to heat things up on planet earth!

## SO, WHY SHOULD WE CARE???

Here's why: If the temperature on earth rises even just a little bit, the ice at the North and South poles will start melting faster, and the level of the oceans will rise. This could flood some of our coastal cities. And higher temperatures could turn some of our best croplands into deserts. This may not happen for a hundred years or more. It may happen in our lifetimes! We still don't know, but many scientists believe saving energy is important.

## BUT WHAT'S A KID TO DO?

Once again, we found that kids can do a lot! We started by listing the kinds of energy we use. Mostly, it's electricity, natural gas, and gasoline. Then we watched ourselves — and our brothers and sisters, and even our parents! — to see how we were wasting it, and how we could use less. And you know what we found out? We can save a ton.

## "Turn Out that Light!"

Electric light bulbs use a lot of energy. The regular light bulb turns more energy into heat than into light! Fluorescent bulbs are more "energy-efficient." That means they make more light with less energy, because less is wasted as heat. But no matter what kind of lights you use, Turn Them Off! when you're not using them. Every time you flick a switch on, a power plant somewhere is burning more fuel! Use natural light whenever you can. Open the window blinds. On a nice day, go outdoors to read a book. If you leave a 100-watt light bulb burning for ten hours, it means you've put almost two pounds of carbon dioxide back in the atmosphere!

New compact fluorescent bulbs use about one fourth as much power to produce the same amount of light.

# KIDS CAN HELP

## Dress for the Weather!

Another big "Energy Bandit" is your air conditioner. Heating or cooling your house puts lots of carbon dioxide in the atmosphere and, as your parents will tell you, costs a lot of money, too! Humans got along for thousands of years without air conditioning, but we're not about to give it up now. Still, we *can* cut back on how much of it we use. The number-one trick is to dress for the weather. If it's a little cool indoors, don't crank up the heater. Put on a sweater instead! If it's too hot indoors, put on shorts and a T-shirt instead of cranking up the air conditioner. It sounds simple, but it will really help the earth (and your parents' pocketbook!).

Air conditioners use different amounts of electricity. My dad says ours uses 500 watts. So every hour we don't use it keeps almost a pound of carbon dioxide out of the air.

# KIDS CAN HELP

## Who's Watching this Program?

The TV is another big energy hog. Now be honest, how many times have you left the TV on when you left the room, with no one there to watch it? A TV can use as much electricity as several 100-watt light bulbs, so turn it off when you're not watching it. That will keep a lot of carbon dioxide out of the air.

## The Four-Wheeled Carbon Factory. . .

One of the biggest energy bandits is your family car! We're not old enough to drive (yet!) but we sure spend a lot of time in the car. Did you know that just one trip to the store and back may put as much as 20 pounds of carbon dioxide into the atmosphere? That's just from burning one gallon of gasoline. What can kids do to help?

# KIDS CAN HELP

## Walk or Bike Wherever You Can!

Don't ask someone to drive you on short trips when you could safely walk or bike. The exercise will be good for you, and you'll be helping the planet, too! Sometimes it's not safe to bike or walk, but you can plan your car trips carefully. Make a list of the places you need to go, and try to make it all in one trip. Or, ride along when your parents or big brother or sister are going near someplace you need to go. When you do take the car, remind the driver to turn off the engine if you're going to be stopped more than a minute. Think about how much carbon dioxide your car puts in the air while you wait at the drive-in window. Wouldn't it be smarter to park the car, turn off the engine, and walk inside? Sometimes it's even quicker!

# Earth Adventure #3:
# Wet and Wild!

We used a lot of energy chasing down the energy bandits, so it was time for a dip in the neighborhood pool! Ahhh, cool, clear water.

But just when we thought we had solved all the problems of the earth, we realized we were up to our necks in another one: Water!

## What's the Problem with Water?

For one thing, we use too much of it! Fresh water comes
from rain and snow, and only so much falls each year.
Sometimes, people use water much faster than rainfall can
replace it. In dry years, there's not enough fresh water for
farmers and factories and people to use. And a lot of that
water is just wasted, by people like me and you!

It was time to become detectives again, and find out how
much water we use in a single week. As usual, we were
amazed!

# HOW MUCH WATER DO I USE?
# HOW MUCH CAN I SAVE?

We found some of this water information at the library. We were amazed at how much water we each could save.

## KIDS CAN HELP

## Water-Saving Tips:

- Don't run the water while you brush your teeth. You'll save five gallons every time!
- You may use up to 10,000 gallons of water a year taking showers. You could cut that in half by using a "low-flow" shower head (check your local hardware store). Or by taking shorter showers!
- Dishwashing can use a lot of water, too. Instead of running the water, fill the sink with clean water to rinse the dishes. This can save up to 25 gallons.
- Don't use the hose to clean sidewalks and driveways. Use a broom instead.

# SO, WE'VE SAVED OUR WATER, RIGHT? WRONG!

The other big problem with water is all the icky stuff we put in it. Solving the water pollution problem is just as important as saving water. What good is a lake or stream full of water if the fish and plants can't live there? It's already starting to happen in many different parts of our country. And all of this water pollution is caused by people, including you and me.

- Water your lawn or garden early in the morning, so the heat won't dry up the water before the plants can get it. And plant things that don't have to be watered so often. Some plants need much less water.
- The toilet uses a lot of water, around five gallons per flush! A lot of toilets have leaks. A leaky toilet can waste over 20,000 gallons of water a year! So we tested the toilets at Casey's house by putting a little food coloring in the tank. Sure enough, a few minutes later, the water in the toilet bowl started turning color, too! We told Casey's dad and he fixed it.
- We looked it up, and even a faucet that has a little drip can waste over 3,000 gallons a year! So we're the Official Leak Detectives in our houses now. This helps the earth, and saves our parents money, too!

## The Energy Bandits Strike Again!
## Acid Rain.

One of the biggest ways we pollute the water is by using so much energy. Remember all the carbon dioxide that goes into the air every time you turn on a light, or ride in a car? Other chemicals go with it, and mix with water in the clouds to make "acid rain," which falls into our lakes and streams. So anything you do to save energy also helps keep our water clean!

# Keep Your Dirt Clean!

Kids and dirt spend a lot of time together! So remember that anything you pour on the ground could end up on you, or in the water you drink, so don't pour strong cleansers or chemicals, oil or gasoline on the ground. We already told you about composting. Using compost instead of chemical fertilizers keeps those chemicals out of our water.

# Earth Adventure #4:
# Home Sweet Habitat!

We felt good about helping keep our water safe and clean. But it reminded us of another big problem. A problem concerning "habitat." Habitat is just a fancy word for a safe place to live, food to eat, a place to sleep in peace.

Different creatures and plants need different places to live —different "habitats." Fish don't live in trees. Some birds can swim, but they don't live underwater. One kind of creature, the human being, has cut down trees and polluted the water so much that many creatures find their own habitats disappearing.

You've probably heard about the problems humans cause by cutting down the tropical rain forests. Animals and plants we don't even have *names* for are disappearing every year! That's one of those big problems people are working on.

# GIVE MOTHER NATURE A PRESENT!

Working together, we can help give nature back at least a little of the habitat we took to build our cities, our neighborhoods, our own backyards. . . .

## Take Aly's Lawn, for Instance!

Aly has this big backyard, lots of green grass to play on, and a couple of trees. But what if you were a bird, or a butterfly. . . . Wouldn't you rather have some bushes to perch on, some flowers to visit, some berries to eat? If we turned just a corner of her yard into a wildlife habitat, we might see more squirrels and birds and butterflies there!

Aly's dad said he wouldn't mind mowing and fertilizing less of that lawn next summer. He agreed to pay for a few plants and seeds (seeds are cheap) to get us started on a backyard home for birds and animals. We promised to do the work of planting them. And we also decided to plant a lot of the same plants in pots on Casey's apartment balcony. We'll tell you about that later. We were ready to get started, but we still had lots of questions. . . .

# What Plants Should We Use?

The next step was finding out what kinds of plants our animal friends can use for food and shelter. Most wild animals prefer the shelter of tall grasses and small shrubs, which give them protection from enemies. Others need special kinds of food from certain flowers, fruits, and seeds. People at the plant store told us about "native" plants. That means plants that grow wild in our area, and don't need a lot of extra water or special care.

We picked plants that bloom at different times of year, so we always have flowers to attract butterflies and hummingbirds. We also found a bush with berries that stay on the plant all winter, and the birds really like that! There are lots of different berry bushes. Find out what kind grows best in your neighborhood. We got a lot of help from the store that sells plants, and we also asked a librarian to help us find the information we needed.

Tall Plants

Bird bath

Native grasses

short plants

Backyard

# KIDS CAN HELP

## Where Do We Start Digging?

We made a plan on paper first. We picked a spot you could watch from the house, just a little area in the corner of the yard. It's better to start small and add to it later, once you learn what works and what doesn't!

We put the tall plants in back, the shorter plants and some native grasses in front. Aly's dad helped us with the digging, and made sure there were no buried electric wires or other underground problems where we wanted to plant. We made a little birdbath from an old flowerpot saucer. The birds like that!

## It Worked!

It took a while for the plants to start growing and blooming, but just a few months later, we started seeing hummingbirds and butterflies checking it out! And next year, we plan to make it even bigger.

# KIDS CAN HELP

## Here's What We Did at Casey's House:

Casey doesn't have a backyard. He lives in an apartment, about three floors up. It's a great view. He has this little patio, so we found some ways to get some interesting critters to come see him there! We got some blooming plants, and a neat berry bush to plant there, and some of the same plants we planted at my house. His neighbor, Mr. Johnson, is really into birds, so he showed us how to build a little bird feeder out of a plastic bottle. We also made another birdbath. It took a while for the word to get around, but the birds make regular visits now, to see what's new for breakfast!

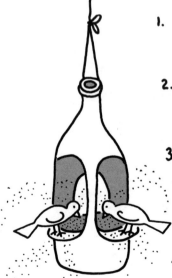

1. Find a plastic bottle and ask an adult to help.

2. Cut holes in sides and bend plastic down.

3. Cut off plastic flap — but leave a little edge for the birds to stand on.

4. Tie a string to the top.

# Earth Adventure #5: Protecting Precious Species™!

We felt pretty good about helping the wild creatures in our neighborhood. But we saw a story on TV about some animals in even bigger trouble! Like elephants, dolphins, whales, cheetahs, turtles.... When creatures are in danger of disappearing, we call them "endangered species." And many more may be in danger soon if we don't make some changes. So this was our next big adventure!

# KIDS CAN HELP

## HOW CAN KIDS PROTECT PRECIOUS SPECIES?

- Don't buy "exotic" pets, which are captured from the wild. Stick to cats and dogs and birds, which are bred locally. For every three wild birds captured, only one will probably live long enough to make it to the pet store!
- Help out with lake, stream, ocean, and highway cleanup projects. Or start one of your own! Plastic trash can kill sea birds and mammals who mistake it for food or get tangled in it.
- When you are fishing or playing in the water, remember all the creatures who live in it! Don't drop scraps of fishing line, plastic six-pack rings, or other trash in the water. And don't dump gasoline in the water.
- Learn all you can about *why* endangered species are endangered. There are lots of books about these species. Then spread the word!

# Earth Adventure #6: Getting the Word Out!

Wow, we found so many ways to start helping right away. But we got to thinking what a difference we could make with some help from our friends! It's important to let your friends and neighbors know you care about the earth. Most folks would care, too, if they just knew what the problems are. So our next puzzle was figuring out how to spread the word. And we learned how loud a few kids' voices can really be!

# KIDS CAN HELP

## Let Everyone Know You Care! Family, Friends, and Neighbors.

We made some posters about saving the earth and put them up at school, and in stores where kids hang out. (We asked permission first, of course.) Casey's dad even took some to his office! Here are some of our ideas, and we know you'll have lots of your own.

1. Save the Dolphins
2. EarthPower — Precycle, Reuse, Recycle
3. Plant a Backyard Habitat
4. Don't Be an Energy Bandit

# POSTER IDEAS

Don't be an ENERGY BANDIT

## Go Write to the Top!

# KIDS CAN HELP

Kids buy a lot of stuff, and the people who run the store and make the products really *do* care what we think. So go right to the top and write letters to business leaders and politicians, even to the President, and tell them what you think. A lot of them write back! What's even better, they will start to make changes if they know we really care.

A lot of the companies we wrote to are already changing the way they do business in order to be gentler to the earth. And local stores will be glad to sell earth-friendly stuff if they know we will buy it: recycled paper products, water and energy saving products, organic gardening products, you name it. You just have to let them know you care! You have to ask them.

Here are some sample letters, to get you started. But feel free to use your own words, and write about things that are important to you!

Dear Store Manager,

We would like to see more products sold in your store that are made of recycled material.

We are telling our friends and neighbors to buy recycled paper products.

Please help us save the planet!

Your friend.
Aly

Dear Mayor,
We are worried about the landfills filling up. We would like to have a recycling pick up in our neighborhood.
Can you help us?

your friend,
Casey

# A LOT OF KIDS WANT TO
# KNOW MORE!

Once we started talking about it, we found a whole bunch
of kids who wanted to help the earth, too. We heard about
a club for kids like us, called Kids for Saving Earth®, so we
started our own KSE club at school. It didn't cost anything
to join, and it was fun to learn that so many other kids are
working to help our planet, too! We found out about a lot
of projects that kids can do together, like adopting a
stream or a park, or planting trees, neighborhood recycling,
composting, and all kinds of things that can really make a
difference! Club members can learn about the causes and
solutions to pollution.


# A LITTLE ABOUT KIDS FOR
# SAVING EARTH®!

Kids for Saving Earth was started by Clinton Hill, an 11-
year-old boy who dreamed of a cleaner, healthier future for
our planet, and he believed that kids could make it happen.
He brought his friends together and they started the Kids
for Saving Earth Club at their school. But soon after, a sad
thing happened. Clinton died of cancer. Today his friends,
his family, and thousands of kids like you around the world
are helping to keep his dream alive. If you'd like to form a
club, write to KSE, Box 47247, Plymouth, MN 55447–0247.

So that's our story. . . so far!

# NOW *YOU* GET STARTED!

# EACH ONE OF US REALLY CAN MAKE THE EARTH A BETTER PLACE FOR ALL LIVING CREATURES, INCLUDING KIDS!

We're still learning new stuff every day, and we hope you will too!! We're sure having fun just checking out our neighborhood pollution problems and we're very proud to help this cool planet called earth.

And you know what? We told our teacher about our earth-saving activities and she plans to take our *whole class* on an earth adventure! Be sure to share your own discoveries with friends, classmates, teachers, and family, too.

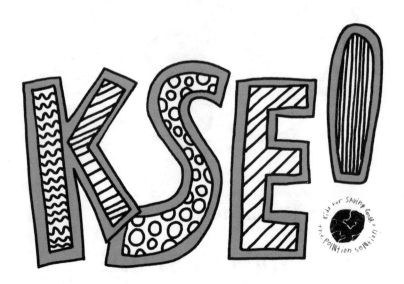